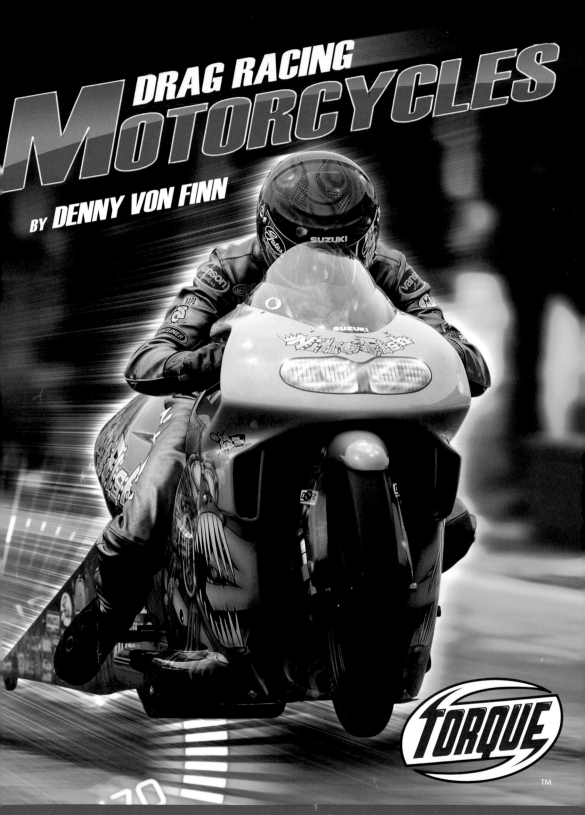

DRAG RACING
MOTORCYCLES

BY DENNY VON FINN

TORQUE™

BELLWETHER MEDIA • MINNEAPOLIS, MN

Are you ready to take it to the extreme?
Torque books thrust you into the action-packed world
of sports, vehicles, and adventure. These books may
include dirt, smoke, fire, and dangerous stunts.
WARNING: read at your own risk.

This edition first published in 2011 by Bellwether Media, Inc.

No part of this publication may be reproduced in whole or in part without written permission of the publisher.
For information regarding permission, write to Bellwether Media, Inc., Attention: Permissions Department,
5357 Penn Avenue South, Minneapolis, MN 55419.

Library of Congress Cataloging-in-Publication Data

Von Finn, Denny.
  Drag racing motorcycles / by Denny Von Finn.
     p. cm. -- (Torque: The world's fastest)
  Includes bibliographical references and index.
  Summary: "Amazing photography accompanies engaging information about drag racing motorcycles.
The combination of high-interest subject matter and light text is intended for students in grades 3 through
7"--Provided by publisher.
  ISBN 978-1-60014-586-5 (hardcover : alk. paper)
  1. Drag bikes--Juvenile literature. I. Title.
  TL442.5V66 2010
  629.227'5--dc22   2010034744

Printed in the United States of America, North Mankato, MN.

010111   1176

CONTENTS

What Are Drag Racing Motorcycles?

Drag racing motorcycles are some of the fastest motorcycles on the planet. They are often called drag bikes. Some can go as fast as 200 miles (322 kilometers) per hour. Races are just 1,320 feet (402 meters) long, but riders need up to 1 mile (1.6 kilometers) to stop after the finish line!

Fast Fact

Michael Phillips set a Pro Stock Motorcycle speed record when he reached 197.65 miles (318.09 kilometers) per hour in 2010.

People race many kinds of drag bikes. With a few **modifications**, everyday motorcycles can compete in drag races. Some riders race **sport bikes**. Others race **V-twins**.

Pro Stock Motorcycle

The fastest drag bikes are Pro Stock Motorcycles. These machines are built just to race. They can go from 0 to 100 miles (161 kilometers) per hour in only a few seconds.

Drag bikes are raced on **drag strips**.
Two riders line their motorcycles up at the
starting line. They watch a tower of lights called
a **Christmas tree**. Three yellow lights blink.
Then the green lights flash! The riders accelerate
down the strip. The first to reach the finish line
is the winner.

Christmas tree

Drag Racing Motorcycle Technology

fork

A lot of advanced technology helps a drag bike reach its incredible speeds. A drag bike is built on a **chassis** of lightweight metal tubing. The front wheel is attached to the chassis with a **fork**. The fork moves up and down to help the tire grip the pavement. This makes the motorcycle more stable during a race.

The drag bike's engine is also attached to the chassis. Some drag bikes have a large V-twin engine. Others have an **inline engine** with four **cylinders**.

Fast Fact

Some drag bikes have a small computer that gathers information about the bike during a race. This information tells the rider's team what modifications will make the bike faster.

Fuel and air are mixed in the engine's cylinders to create power. Pro Stock Motorcycle engines can create 350 **horsepower**. That's about twice as powerful as a normal car engine.

The engine turns the rear wheel when the rider releases the **clutch** at the start of a race. The front wheel rises off the track. Some drag bikes have **wheelie bars**. These extend 10 feet (3 meters) or more off the rear of the bike. They prevent the bike from tipping over backward at the start of a race. Even with wheelie bars, accidents can happen. A rider wears gloves, boots, **leathers**, and a helmet for protection.

Fast Fact

The rear tire on a Pro Stock Motorcycle is 10 inches (25 centimeters) wide. This is wider than a normal motorcycle tire. The extra width helps it grip the track.

wheelie bars

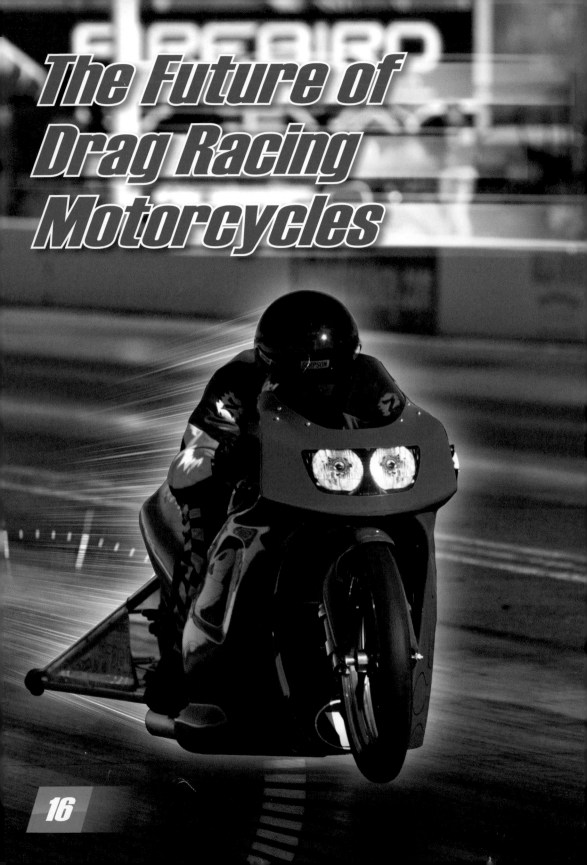

The Future of Drag Racing Motorcycles

Today, more riders are trying motorcycle drag racing than ever before. Drag strips all over the United States host **amateur** motorcycle drag races. Riders don't need expensive Pro Stock Motorcycles. They compete with normal motorcycles. It is a thrilling way to safely test the power of their bikes.

Future drag bikes may be powered by electricity rather than gasoline or **nitromethane**. Over 1,200 small batteries power a drag bike called the KillaCycle.

KillaCycle

The KillaCycle can go from 0 to 60 miles (97 kilometers) per hour in less than one second! It has a top speed of 170 miles (274 kilometers) per hour.

New technology will give drag bikes more power and let riders set new world records. Bikes could use fuels that pollute less than gasoline. The technology could also increase safety.

Drag racing motorcycle riders will always strive for faster speeds. Amateurs and professionals continue to find ways to modify their bikes. They want the fastest bike on the drag strip when the green lights flash!

GLOSSARY

amateur—not professional

chassis—the frame on which a vehicle is built

Christmas tree—a tower of yellow, green, and red lights that help start a drag race

clutch—a device that allows a drag bike's engine to transfer power to the rear wheel

cylinders—hollow chambers inside an engine in which fuel is burned to create power

drag strips—straight, two-lane tracks on which drag bikes race

fork—the part of a motorcycle that connects the front wheel to the chassis

horsepower—a unit used to measure the power of an engine

inline engine—an engine with four cylinders arranged in a straight line

leathers—the suit worn by a drag bike rider

modifications—changes made to a motorcycle to make it faster

nitromethane—an explosive fuel that helps power some drag bikes

sport bikes—motorcycles designed for high speeds and excellent handling

V-twins—motorcycles with engines that have two cylinders arranged in the shape of a "V"

wheelie bars—bars attached to the back of a drag bike that keep the bike from tipping over at the start of a race

TO LEARN MORE

AT THE LIBRARY

David, Jack. *Sport Bikes*. Minneapolis, Minn.: Bellwether Media, 2008.

Von Finn, Denny. *Racing Motorcycles*. Minneapolis, Minn.: Bellwether Media, 2010.

Woods, Bob. *Hottest Motorcycles*. Berkeley Heights, N.J.: Enslow Publishers, 2008.

ON THE WEB

Learning more about
drag racing motorcycles is as easy as 1, 2, 3.

1. Go to www.factsurfer.com.

2. Enter "drag racing motorcycles" into the search box.

3. Click the "Surf" button and you will
   see a list of related Web sites.

With factsurfer.com, finding more information is just a
click away.